The DICTIONARY of
BRAND

PUBLISHED BY

AIGA CENTER FOR BRAND EXPERIENCE

EDITED BY

MARTY NEUMEIER

DESIGNED BY

WILLOUGHBY DESIGN GROUP

THE AIGA PRESS

NEW YORK

For an online version of *The Dictionary of Brand*,
visit www.aiga.org

ISBN # 1-884081-06-1
First edition, published in August 2004 by AIGA

Printed and bound in Canada
by Metropolitan Fine Printers

The AIGA Center for Brand Experience
thanks SMART Papers for contributing
all paper for *The Dictionary of Brand*.

We thank Metropolitan Fine Printers
for donating their time to produce this book.

We also express our gratitude to
the brand experts who generously provided
their advice, time, and ideas to this book.

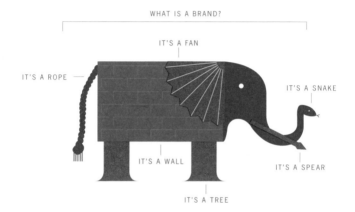

WHAT IS A BRAND?

IT'S A FAN

IT'S A ROPE

IT'S A SNAKE

IT'S A WALL

IT'S A SPEAR

IT'S A TREE

FOREWORD

Why a dictionary of brand? Because brands are increasingly built by specialists, and specialists can only succeed through collaboration. Collaboration, by practical necessity, requires a common language.

Today we find ourselves in the position of the six blind men of Hindustan, unable to describe an elephant except through our separate specialties. The brand is the product, says the product manager. It's the company's reputation, says the PR consultant. The brand is the tagline, says the copywriter. No— it's the visual identity, says the graphic designer. Our brand is our culture, says the CEO. The brand surely derives from functionality, says the engineer. Like the blind men of Hindustan, all of us are partly right, and all of us are wrong.

The Dictionary of Brand is the first step in creating a "linguistic foundation"— a set of terms that allow specialists from different disciplines to work together in a larger community of practice. Neither the terms nor their definitions are carved in stone; we'll most certainly find that many are malleable, some are fluid, and a few are provisionary as we co-develop the practice of brand building.

Although the terms are widely used by brand specialists, most have yet to appear in other dictionaries or glossaries. Of the 221 terms defined here, a fair number were introduced by business authors, in which cases I've tried to include the titles of their books. In fact, if you were to acquire all the books cited in the dictionary, you'd have a good foundation for a brand library.

To help me edit the dictionary, I asked an advisory council made up of experts from various disciplines to lend their thoughts to the project. Outside the council, a number of colleagues from the AIGA Center for Brand Experience helped in herding the right words onto the page. Credit for the design of the book belongs to the Willoughby Design Group. Any mistakes, miscalculations, or misdemeanors belong to me, and will be addressed in later editions. A deep bow to everyone who helped sketch the outlines of the elephant we now call brand.

Marty Neumeier
July 2004

A A A A A A A A A A A A A A A A A A A A A

B B B B B B B B B B B B B B B B B B B B B

C C C C C C C C C C C C C C C C C C C C C

D D D D D D D D D D D D D D D D D D D D D

E E E E E E E E E E E E E E E E E E E E E

F F F F F F F F F F F F F F F F F F F F F

G G G G G G G G G G G G G G G G G G G G G

H H H H H H H H H H H H H H H H H H H H H

I I I I I I I I I I I I I I I I I I I I I

J J J J J J J J J J J J J J J J J J J J J

K K K K K K K K K K K K K K K K K K K K K

L L L L L L L L L L L L L L L L L L L L L

M M M M M M M M M M M M M M M M M M M M M

N N N N N N N N N N N N N N N N N N N N N

O O O O O O O O O O O O O O O O O O O O O

P P P P P P P P P P P P P P P P P P P P P

Q Q Q Q Q Q Q Q Q Q Q Q Q Q Q Q Q Q Q Q Q

R R R R R R R R R R R R R R R R R R R R R

S S S S S S S S S S S S S S S S S S S S S

T T T T T T T T T T T T T T T T T T T T T

U U U U U U U U U U U U U U U U U U U U U

V V V V V V V V V V V V V V V V V V V V V

W W W W W W W W W W W W W W W W W W W W W

X X X X X X X X X X X X X X X X X X X X X

Y Y Y Y Y Y Y Y Y Y Y Y Y Y Y Y Y Y Y Y Y

Z Z Z Z Z Z Z Z Z Z Z Z Z Z Z Z Z Z Z Z Z

ARTIFACT: a visible representation of an idea; a product or by-product of designing | see p.37 designing

ASPIRATIONAL POSITIONING: one or two words which declare what the brand aspires to be in relation to competing brands | see also p.68 mission statement | see p.78 positioning

ATMOSPHERICS: the identity of a brand environment, represented by its architecture, signage, textures, scents, sounds, colors, and employee behavior | see p.43 experience design

ATTITUDE STUDY: a survey of opinions about a brand, often used as a benchmark before and after making changes to it

AUDIENCE: the group to which a product, service, or message is aimed; also called the *target audience*

AUTHENTICITY: the quality of being genuine, often considered a powerful brand attribute

AVATAR: a brand icon designed to move, morph, or otherwise operate freely across various media

see p.53 icon | see p.7 illustration

AWARENESS STUDY: a survey that measures an audience's familiarity with a brand, often divided into "prompted" and "spontaneous" awareness see p.6 audience

AVATAR FOR CINGULAR WIRELESS, KNOWN AS "THE JACK"

BACKSTORY: the story behind
a brand, such as its origin, the
meaning of its name, or the
underpinnings of its authenticity
or charisma | see p.6 authenticity

BENEFIT: a perceived advantage
derived from a product, service,
feature, or attribute

BHAG: a "Big, Hairy, Audacious Goal"
designed to focus an organization

| see *Built to Last*, Jim Collins and Jerry Porras

| see p.42 envisioned future

BOTTOM-UP MARKETING:
customer-driven marketing,
as opposed to top-down or
management-driven marketing

| see *Bottom-Up Marketing*, Al Ries and Jack Trout

BRA

ND:

a person's
perception
of a
product, service,
experience or
organization;

the **art** and
science of
brand-
building

BRAND: a person's perception
of a product, service, experience
or organization; the art and
science of brand building

BRAND AGENCY: a strategic firm
that provides or manages a variety
of brand-building services across
a range of media

BRAND ALIGNMENT: the practice
of linking brand strategy to customer
touchpoints see p.27 brand strategy

see p.96 touchpoint

BRAND AMBASSADOR: anyone
who promotes the brand through
interactions with customers,
prospects, partners, or the media;
ideally, every company employee

BRAND ARCHITECTURE: a hierarchy of related brands, often beginning with a master brand, describing its relationship to subbrands and co-brands; a brand family tree | see p.66 master brand

| see p.92 subbrand | see p.31 co-branding | see illustration below

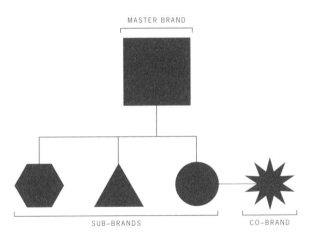

MASTER BRAND

SUB-BRANDS

CO-BRAND

BRAND ARTICULATION: a concise description of a brand that enables members of the brand community to collaborate; the brand story

| see p.17 brand community | see p.27 brand story

BRAND ASSET: any aspect of a brand that has strategic value, which may include brand associations, brand attributes, brand awareness, or brand loyalty | see p.16 brand attribute

| see p.21 brand loyalty

BRAND ATTRIBUTE: a distinctive feature of a product, service, company, or brand

BRAND AUDIT: a formal assessment of a brand's strengths and weaknesses across all of its touchpoints | see p.96 touchpoint

BRAND CHAMPION: anyone who evangelizes or protects a brand; a brand steward | see p.25 brand steward

BRAND COMMUNITY: the network of people who contribute to building a brand, including internal departments, external firms, industry partners, customers, users, and the media

BRAND CONSULTANT: an external adviser who contributes to the brand-building process, often in a strategic or advisory role

BRAND COUNCIL: a committee formed to assess and guide a company's brand-building process; sometimes called a *creative council*

BRAND DESIGNER: any person who helps shape a brand, including graphic designers, strategists, marketing directors, researchers, advertising planners, web developers, public relations specialists, copywriters, and others

BRAND EARNINGS: the share of a business's cashflow that can be attributed to the brand alone

BRANDED HOUSE: a company in which the dominant brand name is the company name, such as Mercedes-Benz; also called a *homogeneous brand* or a *monolithic brand* | see p.51 the opposite of a house of brands

BRAND EQUITY: the accumulated
value of a company's brand assets,
both financially and strategically; the
overall market strength of a brand

| see *Managing Brand Equity*, David A. Aaker

BRAND ESSENCE: the distillation
of a brand's promise into the
simplest possible terms | see illustration below

BRAND NAME

BRAND NAME	BRAND ESSENCE
CHRYSLER	nostalgic american cars
HEWLETT–PACKARD	inventive technology
IKEA	cheap modular furniture
KODAK	family memories
PORSCHE	performance sports cars
OIL OF OLAY	younger skin
WELLS FARGO	historic bank

BRAND ESSENCE

BRAND EXPERIENCE: all the interactions people have with a product, service, or organization; the raw material of a brand

see p.27 brand story

BRAND GAP: the gulf between business strategy and customer experience | see *The Brand Gap*, Marty Neumeier

BRAND IDENTITY: the outward expression of a brand, including its name, trademark, communications, and visual appearance

see *Designing Brand Identity*, Alina Wheeler

BRAND IMAGE: a customer's mental picture of a product, service, or organization

BRANDING: any effort or program
to build a brand; the process of
brand-building

BRAND LOYALTY: the strength
of preference for a brand compared
to competing brands, sometimes
measured in repeat purchases

BRAND MANAGER: an obsoles-
cent term for a person responsible
for tactical issues facing a brand
or brand family, such as pricing,
promotion, distribution, and
advertising; a product manager

BRAND MANUAL: a document that
articulates the parameters of the
brand for members of the brand
community; a standardized set of
brand-building tools | see p.17 brand community

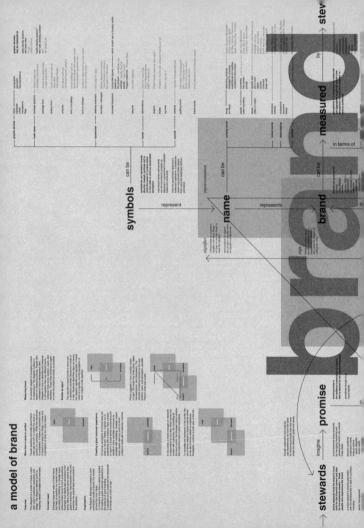

a model of brand

Overview

Measuring brand

Concept image

Brand as signs

Organization

More than a name or symbol

Creating a great customer experience

symbols — can be — represent → name

name — represents → brand

brand — can be — measured — in terms of

by → stev

stewards → imagine → promise → ...

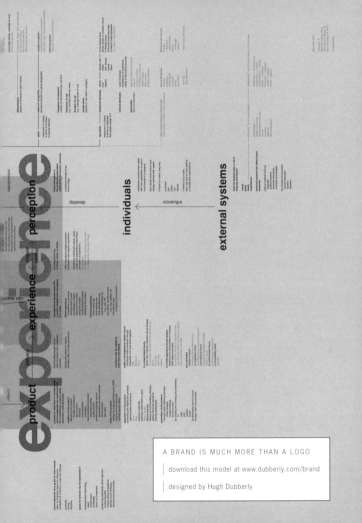

A BRAND IS MUCH MORE THAN A LOGO

download this model at www.dubberly.com/brand

designed by Hugh Dubberly

BRANDMARK: an icon, avatar, wordmark or other symbol for a brand; a trademark | see p.53 icon

| see p.6 avatar | see p.105 wordmark | see p.92 symbol

| see p.97 trademark

BRAND METRICS: measurements for monitoring changes in brand equity | see p.27 brand valuation

BRAND NAME: the verbal or written component of a brand icon; the name of a product, service, experience, or organization

| see p.53 icon

BRAND PERSONALITY:

the character of a brand as defined in human terms, such as Virgin = irreverent, or Chanel = refined

BRAND POLICE: manager or team responsible for strict compliance with the guidelines in the brand manual | see p.21 brand manual

BRAND PORTFOLIO: a suite of related brands; a collection of brands owned by one company

| see *Brand Portfolio Strategy*, David A. Aaker

BRAND PUSHBACK: marketplace resistance to brand messages or brand extensions, often leading to changes in brand strategy

| see p.43 extension | see p.27 brand strategy

BRAND STEWARD: the person responsible for developing and protecting a brand

WITHOUT THE BRAND,
COKE'S GLASS WOULD
BE HALF EMPTY

COKE'S MARKET CAP.
INCLUDING BRAND VALUE:
$120 BILLION

COKE'S MARKET CAP.
NOT INCLUDING BRAND VALUE:
$50 BILLION

source | Interbrand Top 100 Brands

BRAND STORY: the articulation of a brand as a narrative; a coherent set of messages that articulate the meaning of a brand | also see p.9 backstory

BRAND STRATEGY: a plan for the systematic development of a brand in order to meet business objectives

BRAND VALUATION: the process of measuring the monetary equity of a brand | also see p.24 brand metrics

BUZZ: the current public opinion about a product, service, experience, or organization | see *The Anatomy of Buzz*,

Emanuel Rosen

CATEGORY: the arena in which a
brand competes; a consideration set

| see p.32 consideration set

CBO: a company's Chief Brand
Officer, responsible for integrating
the work of the brand community

| see p.17 brand community

CHALLENGER BRAND: a new
or rising brand that is viable in
spite of competition from the
dominant brand in its category

| see *Eating the Big Fish*, Adam Morgan

CHARISMATIC BRAND: a brand
that inspires a high degree of
loyalty; also known as a *lifestyle
brand* or *passion brand* | see p.97 tribal brand

CLUTTER: the conceptual noise of the marketplace; a disorderly array of messages or elements that impedes understanding | see illustration below

CO-BRANDING: the purposeful linking of two or more brands for mutual benefit

CO-CREATION: the collaborative development of a product, service, brand, or message

COLLABORATION: the process by which people of different disciplines work in concert to build a brand; the practice of co-creation | see *Serious Play*, and *No More Teams!*, Michael Schrage

COMMAND AND CONTROL: a management style relying on clearly defined goals, processes, and measurements; top-down rather than distributed or bottom-up management

COMMODITIZATION: the process
by which customers come to see
products, services, or companies
as interchangeable, resulting
in the erosion of profit margins;
the opposite of brand-building

| see p.102 vicious circle

CONCEPT MAP: a diagram
showing the connections among
a set of concepts

CONCEPTUAL NOISE: cognitive
clutter arising from too many messages
or meanings; any competing ideas
that undermine clarity | see p.30 clutter

CONSIDERATION SET: the range
of brands that a customer considers
when making a purchase decision;
a category | see p.29 category

CORE COMPETENCIES: a set of
capabilities (typically two or three)
that gives a company a strategic
advantage

CORE IDENTITY: the central,
sustainable elements of a brand
identity, usually the name and
trademark | see p.20 brand identity | see p.97 trademark

CORE IDEOLOGY: a combination
of core values and core purpose

| see p.34 core values | see p.34 core purpose

CORE IDEOLOGY

CORE VALUES

CORE PURPOSE

VISION

B.H.A.G.

VIVID DESCRIPTION

ENVISIONED FUTURE

source | Jim Collins and Jerry Porras, *Harvard Business Review OnPoint*

CORE PURPOSE: the reason a company exists beyond making a profit; part of a core ideology

| see illustration p.33 | see p.33 core ideology

CORE VALUES: an enduring set of principles that defines the ethics of a company; part of a core ideology

| see illustration p.33 | see p.33 core ideology

CORPORATE IDENTITY: the brand identity of a company, consisting of its visual identifiers such as the name, trademark, typography, and colors; a company's trade dress | see p.20 brand identity

| see p.96 trade dress

CREATIVE BRIEF: a document that sets parameters for a brand-building project, including context, goals, processes, and budgetary constraints

CULTIVATION: the process of
imbedding brand values throughout
the organization; internal branding

| see p.55 internal branding | see *Building the Brand-Driven Business*,

Scott M. Davis and Michael Dunn

CULTURE JAMMING: the act of
modifying advertisements or brand
messages to subvert their original
intent; also known as *subvertising*

| see *Adbusters* magazine

CUSTOMER EXPECTATIONS:
the anticipated benefits of a brand,
whether explicit or implicit

CUSTOMER GOALS: the "jobs"
that customers "hire" a product,
service, experience, or organization
to do for them | see *The Innovator's Solution*,

Clayton M. Christensen and Michael E. Raynor

A A A A A A A A A A A A A A A A A A A A A
B B B B B B B B B B B B B B B B B B B B B
C C C C C C C C C C C C C C C C C C C C C
D D D D D D D D D D D D D D D D D D D
E E E E E E E E E E E E E E E E E E E E E
F F F F F F F F F F F F F F F F F F F F F
G G G G G G G G G G G G G G G G G G G G G
H H H H H H H H H H H H H H H H H H H H H
I I I I I I I I I I I I I I I I I I I I I
J J J J J J J J J J J J J J J J J J J J J
K K K K K K K K K K K K K K K K K K K K K
L L L L L L L L L L L L L L L L L L L L L
M M M M M M M M M M M M M M M M M M M M M
N N N N N N N N N N N N N N N N N N N N N
O O O O O O O O O O O O O O O O O O O O O
P P P P P P P P P P P P P P P P P P P P P
Q Q Q Q Q Q Q Q Q Q Q Q Q Q Q Q Q Q Q Q Q
R R R R R R R R R R R R R R R R R R R R R
S S S S S S S S S S S S S S S S S S S S S
T T T T T T T T T T T T T T T T T T T T T
U U U U U U U U U U U U U U U U U U U U U
V V V V V V V V V V V V V V V V V V V V V
W W W W W W W W W W W W W W W W W W W W W
X X X X X X X X X X X X X X X X X X X X X
Y Y Y Y Y Y Y Y Y Y Y Y Y Y Y Y Y Y Y Y Y
Z Z Z Z Z Z Z Z Z Z Z Z Z Z Z Z Z Z Z Z Z

DESCRIPTOR: a term used with
a brand name to describe the
category in which the brand competes, such as "fluoride toothpaste"
or "online bank" | see p.29 category

DESIGN: in brand-building, the
planning or shaping of products,
services, environments, systems,
communications, or other artifacts
to create a positive brand experience

| see p.5 artifact

DESIGNING: the process of design;
bringing together strategic and creative
processes to achieve a shared goal

| see design above | see *Why Design?*, published by AIGA

DESIGN MANAGEMENT:
the practice of integrating the work of internal and external design teams to align brand expressions with strategic goals

DESIGN RESEARCH: customer research on the experience and design of products or communication elements, using qualitative, quantitative, or ethnographic techniques | see p.83 qualitative | see p.83 quantitative | see p.42 ethnography | also see p.45 field test | also see p.47 focus group | also see p.65 mall intercept | also see p.75 one-on-one interview

DIFFERENTIATION: the process of establishing a unique market position to increase profit margins and avoid commoditization; the result of positioning | see p.32 commoditization | see p.78 positioning | see *Differentiate or Die*, Jack Trout

DISRUPTIVE INNOVATION:

a new product, service, or business that redefines the market; also called *discontinuous innovation* | see *The Innovator's Dilemma*, Clayton Christensen | see p.47 first mover

DRIVE FEATURES: brand attributes

that are both important to customers and highly differentiated from those of competitors | see p.16 brand attribute

| see *The McKinsey Quarterly*, May 2004

DRIVER BRAND: in a brand

portfolio, the brand that drives a purchase decision, whether master brand, sub-brand, or endorser brand

| see p.25 brand portfolio | see p.66 master brand
| see p.92 subbrand | see p.42 endorser brand

EARCON: an auditory brand
symbol, such as United Airlines'
use of "Rhapsody in Blue" as a brand
expression; an aural icon | see p.53 icon

ELEVATOR PITCH: a one-sentence
version of a brand's purpose or
market position, short enough to
convey during a brief elevator ride

| see p.66 market position

EMERGENT ATTRIBUTE:
a feature, benefit, quality,
or experience that arises from
the brand, as opposed to the core
product or service; an example
is the friendliness of Google

EMOTIONAL BRANDING: brand-
building efforts that aim at customers'
feelings through sensory experiences

| see *Emotional Branding*, Marc Gobé

ENDORSER BRAND: a brand that
promises satisfaction on behalf of
a subbrand or co-brand, usually in
a secondary position to the brand
being endorsed | see p.92 subbrand

| see p.31 co-branding

ENVISIONED FUTURE: a 10- to
30-year BHAG with vivid descrip-
tions of what it will be like to reach
the goal | see p.9 BHAG | see p.103 vivid description

| see *Built to Last,* Jim Collins and Jerry Porras

ETHNOGRAPHY: the study of
people in their natural settings;
research to discover needs and
desires that can be met with
brand innovations

EXPERIENCE DESIGN: a focus
on shaping the experience of a
customer or user, rather than on the
artifacts themselves; the design of
interactive media | see p.5 artifact

| also see p.43 information architect

EXTENDED IDENTITY: the
elements that extend the core
identity of a company or brand,
organized into groupings such as
brand personality, symbols, and
positioning | see p.33 core identity | see p.24
brand personality | see p.92 symbol | see p.78 positioning

EXTENSION: a new product or
service that leverages the brand
equity of a related product or service

EVANGELIST: a brand advocate,
whether paid or unpaid

A A A A A A A A A A A A A A A A A A A A A

B B B B B B B B B B B B B B B B B B B B B

C C C C C C C C C C C C C C C C C C C C C

D D D D D D D D D D D D D D D D D D D D D

E E E E E E E E E E E E E E E E E E E E E

F F F F F F F F F F F F F F F F F F F F

G G G G G G G G G G G G G G G G G G G G

H H H H H H H H H H H H H H H H H H H H H

I I I I I I I I I I I I I I I I I I I I I

J J J J J J J J J J J J J J J J J J J J J

K K K K K K K K K K K K K K K K K K K K K

L L L L L L L L L L L L L L L L L L L L L

M M M M M M M M M M M M M M M M M M M M

N N N N N N N N N N N N N N N N N N N N N

O O O O O O O O O O O O O O O O O O O O O

P P P P P P P P P P P P P P P P P P P P P

Q Q Q Q Q Q Q Q Q Q Q Q Q Q Q Q Q Q Q Q Q

R R R R R R R R R R R R R R R R R R R R R

S S S S S S S S S S S S S S S S S S S S S

T T T T T T T T T T T T T T T T T T T T

U U U U U U U U U U U U U U U U U U U U U

V V V V V V V V V V V V V V V V V V V V V

W W W W W W W W W W W W W W W W W W W W

X X X X X X X X X X X X X X X X X X X X X

Y Y Y Y Y Y Y Y Y Y Y Y Y Y Y Y Y Y Y Y Y

Z Z Z Z Z Z Z Z Z Z Z Z Z Z Z Z Z Z Z Z Z

FEATURE: any element of a product, service, or experience designed to deliver a benefit

FEATURE CREEP: the addition of unnecessary elements to a product, service, or experience; sometimes called *featuritis*

FIELD TEST: qualitative research used to assess a new product, package, concept, or message

see p.83 qualitative research

FIFTH DISCIPLINE: the organizational discipline of systems thinking, used to integrate four other disciplines: personal mastery, mental models, shared vision, and team learning

see *The Fifth Discipline*, Peter Senge

THE APPLE iPOD, A FIRST MOVER

FIRST MOVER: a company or brand
that leads a new category | see p.39

disruptive innovation | see illustration p.46

FOCUS GROUP: a qualitative
research technique in which several
people are invited to a research
facility to discuss a given subject;
a type of research designed to focus
later research | see p.83 qualitative research

FOLLOWSHIP: the art of building on
collaborators' ideas; the opposite of
NIH syndrome | see p.72 NIH syndrome

FUTURECASTING: a technique
used to envision future products,
industries, competitors, challenges,
or opportunities; a combination of
forecasting and imagination

| see *Unstuck*, Keith Yamashita and Sandra Spataro, Ph.D.

GENERIC: an unbranded product, service, or experience; a commodity

| see p.32 commoditization

GENERIC BRAND: a misnomer often applied to a commodity product or store brand (since the terms generic and brand are mutually exclusive) | see p.91 store brand

GLOBAL BRAND: a product, service, or company that competes globally (often a misnomer, since most brands, by definition, vary from culture to culture)

GUERILLA MARKETING: a marketing program that uses non-traditional channels to sell or advertise products or services

| see *Guerilla Marketing*, Jay Conrad Levinson

HARMONIZATION: the alignment
of the elements of a brand across
product lines or geographic regions

HAWTHORNE EFFECT:
the tendency for research subjects
to behave uncharacteristically

see p.75 observer effect

HOLLYWOOD MODEL: a system
of creative collaboration in which
specialists work as a team for the
duration of a project also see p.54 IMT

also see p.68 metateam | also see p.102 virtual agency

HOUSE OF BRANDS: a company
in which the dominant brand names
are those of the products and services
the company sells, also called a
heterogeneous brand or *pluralistic brand*

see p.18 opposite of a branded house

ICON: the visual symbol of a brand,
usually based on a differentiated
market position; a trademark

see p.97 trademark | see illustration above

IMT: an Integrated Marketing Team, comprised of various specialist firms working in collaboration to build a brand; a metateam or virtual agency

see p.68 metateam | see p.102 virtual agency

also see p.51 Hollywood model

INFORMATION ARCHITECT: a person who designs complex information systems to make them more navigable | see *Information Architects*, edited by Richard Saul Wurman

INFORMATION HIERARCHY: the order of importance of the elements in a brand message

INGREDIENT BRAND: a brand used as a selling feature in another brand

INNOVATION: a market-changing product, service, experience, or concept; the formal practice of innovation | see *The Art of Innovation*, Tom Kelley

INTEGRATED MARKETING: a collaborative method for developing consistent messaging across media

INTELLECTUAL PROPERTY: intangible assets protected by patents and copyrights; the legal discipline that specializes in the protection of brand assets, including brand names, trademarks, colors, shapes, sounds, and smells

INTERNAL BRANDING: an internal program to spread brand understanding through the use of standards manuals, orientation sessions, workshops, critiques, and online training; brand cultivation

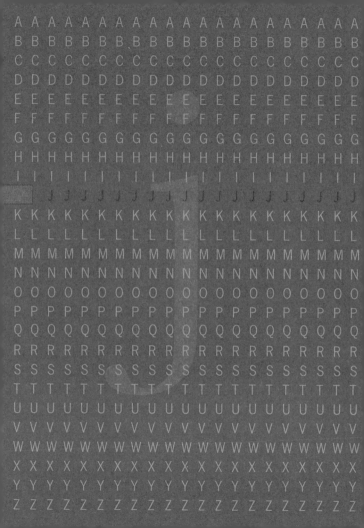

JAMMING: building a brand or company through improvisational collaboration | see *Jamming*, John Kao

| see illustration below

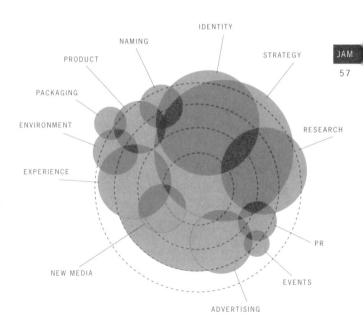

IDENTITY

NAMING

PRODUCT

STRATEGY

PACKAGING

ENVIRONMENT

RESEARCH

EXPERIENCE

PR

NEW MEDIA

EVENTS

ADVERTISING

A A A A A A A A A A A A A A A A A A A A A
B B B B B B B B B B B B B B B B B B B B B
C C C C C C C C C C C C C C C C C C C C C
D D D D D D D D D D D D D D D D D D D D D
E E E E E E E E E E E E E E E E E E E E E
F F F F F F F F F F F F F F F F F F F F F
G G G G G G G G G G G G G G G G G G G G G
H H H H H H H H H H H H H H H H H H H H H
I I I I I I I I I I I I I I I I I I I I I
J J J J J J J J J J J J J J J J J J J J J
K K K K K K K K K K K K K K K K K K K K
L L L L L L L L L L L L L L L L L L L L L
M M M M M M M M M M M M M M M M M M M M M
N N N N N N N N N N N N N N N N N N N N N
O O O O O O O O O O O O O O O O O O O O O
P P P P P P P P P P P P P P P P P P P P P
Q Q Q Q Q Q Q Q Q Q Q Q Q Q Q Q Q Q Q Q Q
R R R R R R R R R R R R R R R R R R R R R
S S S S S S S S S S S S S S S S S S S S S
T T T T T T T T T T T T T T T T T T T T T
U U U U U U U U U U U U U U U U U U U U U
V V V V V V V V V V V V V V V V V V V V V
W W W W W W W W W W W W W W W W W W W W W
X X X X X X X X X X X X X X X X X X X X X
Y Y Y Y Y Y Y Y Y Y Y Y Y Y Y Y Y Y Y Y Y
Z Z Z Z Z Z Z Z Z Z Z Z Z Z Z Z Z Z Z Z Z

KIT OF PARTS: a complete brand identity scheme, including name, trademark, typography, colors, shapes, sound signatures, taglines, and other expressions of the brand

| see p.20 brand identity | see illustration below

LEVERAGING A BRAND: borrowing
   from the credibility of one brand
   to launch another brand, subbrand,
   or co-brand; brand extension | see p.92

subbrand | see p.31 co-branding | see below line extension

LINE EXTENSION: the addition
   of one or more subbrands to a master
   brand; the expansion of a brand
   family | see p.53 subbrands | see p.53 master brand

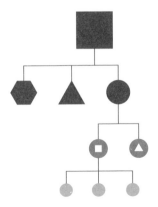

LIVING BRAND: a brand that grows, changes, and sustains itself; a healthy brand

LOGO: an abbreviation of logotype, now applied broadly (if incorrectly) to all trademarks | see below logotype

LOGOTYPE: a distinctive typeface or lettering style used to represent a brand name; a wordmark

| see p.105 wordmark

LOOK AND FEEL: the sensory experience of a product, environment, or communication

ICON
SYMBOL
AVATAR.

LOGOTYPE
WORDMARK

 TARGET

TRADEMARK
BRANDMARK
SIGNATURE

THE PARTS OF A TRADEMARK

MALL INTERCEPT: a market
research technique in which
researchers interview customers in
a store or public location; a one-on-
one interview | see p.75 one-on-one interview

MARKETING: the process of
developing, promoting, selling, and
distributing a product or service

| see *The 22 Immutable Laws of Marketing*, Al Ries

MARKETING AESTHETICS:
the principles of perception used to
enhance the feelings or experiences
of an audience | see p.77 perception | see p.6 audience

| see *Marketing Aesthetics*, Bernd Schmitt and Alex Simonson

MARKET PENETRATION:
the market share of a product,
service, or company compared to
others in the category

MARKET POSITION: the ranking of a product, service, or company within a category, sometimes calculated as market share multiplied by share of mind | also see positioning p.78

MARKET SHARE: the percentage of total sales in a given category, usually expressed in the number of units sold or the value of units sold

| also see market position above

MASTER BRAND: the dominant brand in a line or across a business, such as Pepperidge Farm or Sony, to which subbrands can be added; a parent brand | see p.92 subbrand | see p.77 parent brand | also see brand architecture p.15

MEDIA: the channels through which brand messages are delivered, such as television, printed publications, direct mail, the Internet, and outdoor posters

MEDIA ADVERTISING: one-way messages designed to sell, persuade, or create awareness of a brand through public communication channels

MEME: an idea that self-reproduces like a virus; a unit of social currency, such as "Where's the beef?" or "Sweet!" | see *The Selfish Gene*, Richard Dawkins

| see illustration below

I♥NY is a registered trademark and service mark of the New York State Department of Economic Development; used with permission.

MENTAL MODEL: a conceptual image of an experience, environment, process, or system that provides better understanding or predictive value

MESSAGE ARCHITECTURE: the formal relationships among brand communications

METATEAM: a large team made up of smaller specialist teams; an IMT or virtual agency | see p.54 IMT

| see p.102 virtual agency | also see p.51 Hollywood model

MISSION STATEMENT: a concise statement of the purpose or aspirations of an organization

MORPHEME: the smallest unit of language that has meaning, often used by naming specialists to assemble coined words, or neologisms | see p.71 neologism | see illustration below

○ excel	○ adven	○ prov	○ sis	○ nia	○ sys
○ arri	○ insig	○ daig	○ ra	○ ren	○ ori
○ utop	○ inno	○ arch	○ iva	○ o	● ete
○ centr	○ oft	○ alta	○ ten	○ tior	○ rogy
○ assa	○ dyni	○ centri	⊘ ent	○ igo	○ geo
○ syns	○ tria	○ alam	○ isa	○ ean	○ pia
○ net	○ cali	⊘ agil	○ ete	○ se	○ rus
○ futu	○ imar	○ seni	○ ili	○ ara	○ va

source | *SOON; Brands of Tommorrow*, Lewis Blackworth and Chris Ashworth

NAME BRAND: a widely recognized product, service, or organization

NATURAL READING SEQUENCE: the order in which readers can most easily absorb separate pieces of information

NEOLOGISM: a coined word or phrase that can serve as a brand name

| see also p.69 morpheme

NEW LUXURY: goods and services that deliver higher quality or superior performance at a premium price, such as Belvedere Vodka or Callaway Golf Clubs | see *Trading Up*, Michael J. Silverstein and Neil Fiske

NIH SYNDROME: the tendency of a company, department, employee, or consultant to reject any idea "Not Invented Here"

NO-LOGO MOVEMENT: a group of activists who see global brands as a form of cultural imperialism

see *No Logo*, Naomi Klein

NOMENCLATURE SYSTEM: a formal structure for naming related products, services, features, or benefits; the naming portion of an organization's brand architecture

see p.15 brand architecture | see illustration p.73

FLAGSHIP NAMES

CitiBusiness®

CitiGold®

CitiDirect®

CitiSelect®

5% OF ALL NAMES

95% OF ALL NAMES

DESCRIPTIVE NAMES

Citi® Trust Services

Citi® Auto Payment

Citibank® Money Market Account

73

NOMENCLATURE FOR THE CITI BRAND

OBSERVER EFFECT: a tendency in which the presence of the observer changes what is being observed

see p.51 Hawthorne effect

ONE-ON-ONE INTERVIEW: a market research technique in which subjects are interviewed one at a time

ONE-STOP SHOP: a single firm that offers a full range of branding services, as opposed to an IMT

see p.54 IMT

OPINION LEADER: a person whose opinion or personality exerts an influence over other members of a group; also called an *opinion maker*

PARALLEL EXECUTION:
the process by which creative teams work simultaneously rather than sequentially

PARALLEL THINKING: a brainstorming technique in which everyone thinks in the same direction at the same time, generating a range of usable ideas; the opposite of Socratic thinking, in which one person succeeds by proving the other wrong

| see *Six Thinking Hats*, Edward de Bono

PARENT BRAND: the main brand in a brand family; a master brand

| see p.66 master brand | also see p.15 brand architecture

PERCEPTION: an impression received through the senses; a building block of customer experience

| also see p.65 marketing aesthetics

PERCEPTUAL MAP: a diagram of customer perceptions showing the relationships between competing products, service, companies, or brands

PERMANENT MEDIA: environmental brand messages that last for years, such as architecture or signage

PERMISSION MARKETING: the practice of promoting goods or services with anticipated, personal, and relevant messages

| see *Permission Marketing*, Seth Godin

POSITIONING: the process of differentiating a product, service, or company in a customer's mind to obtain a strategic competitive advantage; the first step in building a brand | see *Positioning*, Al Ries and Jack Trout

POWER LAW: in brand building,
the tendency for success to attract
more success; a law that explains
why the "rich get richer"

see p.103 virtuous circle | see illustration below

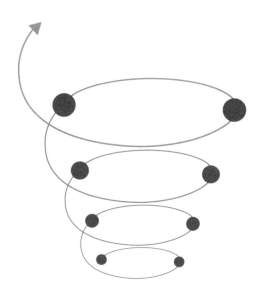

PRIMACY EFFECT: the observation that first impressions tend to be stronger than later impressions, except for last impressions | see p.85 recency effect

PRIVATE LABEL: a store-owned product that competes, often at a lower price, with widely distributed products; a store brand as opposed to a name brand | see p.91 store brand
| see p.71 name brand

PRODUCT PLACEMENT: a form of paid advertising in which products and trademarks are inserted into non-advertising media such as movies, television programs, music, and public environments

PROMISE: a stated or implied pledge that creates customer expectations and employee responsibilities, such as FedEx's on-time guarantee

PROSUMER: a category of products and services that combines professional-level features with consumer-level usability and price

PROTOTYPE: a model, mockup, or plan used to evaluate or develop a new product, service, environment, communication, or experience

PURE PLAY: a company with a single line of business; a highly focused brand

A A A A A A A A A A A A A A A A A A A A A A A
B B B B B B B B B B B B B B B B B B B B B B
C C C C C C C C C C C C C C C C C C C C C C
D D D D D D D D D D D D D D D D D D D D D D
E E E E E E E E E E E E E E E E E E E E E E E
F F F F F F F F F F F F F F F F F F F F F F F
G G G G G G G G G G G G G G G G G G G G G G
H H H H H H H H H H H H H H H H H H H H H H
I I I I I I I I I I I I I I I I I I I I I I I
J J J J J J J J J J J J J J J J J J J J J J
K K K K K K K K K K K K K K K K K K K K K K
L L L L L L L L L L L L L L L L L L L L L L
M M M M M M M M M M M M M M M M M M M M M
N N N N N N N N N N N N N N N N N N N N N N
O O O O O O O O O O O O O O O O O O O O O O
P P P P P P P P P P P P P P P P P P P P P P
Q Q Q Q Q Q Q Q Q Q Q Q Q Q Q Q Q Q Q Q Q
R R R R R R R R R R R R R R R R R R R R R R
S S S S S S S S S S S S S S S S S S S S S S
T T T T T T T T T T T T T T T T T T T T T T
U U U U U U U U U U U U U U U U U U U U U U
V V V V V V V V V V V V V V V V V V V V V V
W W W W W W W W W W W W W W W W W W W W W
X X X X X X X X X X X X X X X X X X X X X X
Y Y Y Y Y Y Y Y Y Y Y Y Y Y Y Y Y Y Y Y Y Y
Z Z Z Z Z Z Z Z Z Z Z Z Z Z Z Z Z Z Z Z Z Z

QUALITATIVE RESEARCH:
research designed to provide insight,
such as one-on-one interviews and
focus groups | see p.75 one-on-one interviews

| see p.47 focus groups | also see p.38 design research

PERCEPTION

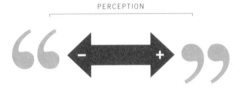

QUANTITATIVE RESEARCH:
research designed to provide measure-
ment, such as polling and large-scale
studies | also see p.38 design research

RAPID PROTOTYPING: a process of producing quick rounds of mockups, models, or concepts in rapid succession, evaluating and reiterating after each round to develop more effective products, services, or experiences

| see *The Art of Innovation*, Tom Kelley

REACH: the number of people exposed to an advertising or brand message | also see p.65 market penetration

RECENCY EFFECT: the observation that last impressions tend to be stronger than earlier impressions, including first impressions

| also see p.80 primacy effect

REPUTATION: the shared opinion of a product, service, or organization among all the members of its audience

| see p.6 audience | also see p.14 brand for comparison

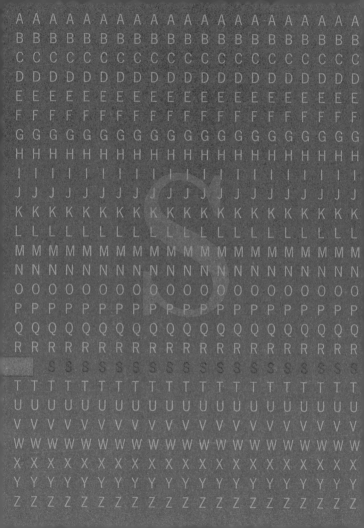

SACRIFICE: the practice of
  eliminating any product, service,
  or feature that fails to strengthen
  a market position or brand

SALES CYCLE: for buyers, the
  steps in making a purchase (often
  defined as awareness, consideration,
  decision, and use); for sellers, the
  steps in making a sale (often defined
  as finding and qualifying customers,
  defining the products or services,
  and accepting and acknowledging
  the order) | see illustration below

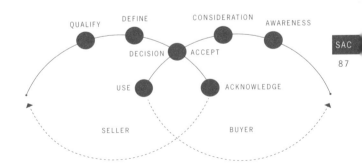

SEGMENT: a group of people who are likely to respond to a given marketing effort in a similar way

| also see p.6 audience

SEGMENTATION: the process of dividing a market into subcategories of people who share similar values and goals

SHELF IMPACT: the ability of a product, package, or brand to stand out on a shelf by virtue of its design

SIGNATURE: the defined visual relationship between a logotype and a symbol | see p.62 logotype | see p.92 symbol

SILO: a department separated from other departments according to product, service, function, or market; a disparaging term for a non-collaborative department

SLOGAN: a catchphrase, tagline, or rally cry | from the Gaelic "sluagh-ghairm," meaning "war cry"

SOCK–PUPPET MARKETING: a disparaging term for "fake" brands built on frothy advertising campaigns, such as those of the dot-com era

| see *The Fall of Advertising*, Al Ries and Laura Ries

SPEECH–STREAM VISIBILITY: the quality of a brand name that allows it to be recognized as a proper noun (as opposed to a generic word) in conversation, such as Kodak or Smuckers

SPECIALIZATION: the strategy of focusing and deepening a business offering to better compete with larger companies, or to better collaborate with other specialists

BUSINESS STRATEGY

BRAND STRATEGY

STRATEGIC DNA

STAKEHOLDER: any person
or firm with a vested interest
in a company or brand, including
shareholders, employees, partners,
suppliers, customers, and
community members

STORE BRAND: a private-label
product that can be sold at lower
prices or higher margins than their
widely distributed competitors,
sometimes incorrectly called generic
brands; a private-label brand

| see p.49 generic brands | see p.80 private label

SOCIAL NETWORK: a network
of people that can be leveraged to
spread ideas or messages using viral
marketing techniques | see p.102 viral marketing

STRATEGIC DNA: a decision-
making code derived from the
intertwining of business strategy
and brand strategy | see illustration p.90

STRATEGY: a plan that uses a set of tactics to achieve a business goal, often by out-maneuvering competitors | also see p.27 brand strategy

SUBBRAND: a secondary brand that builds on the associations of a master brand | see p.66 master brand

SUSTAINING INNOVATION: an incremental improvement to an existing product, service, or business

| also see p.39 disruptive innovation

SWOT: a conceptual tool that analyzes Strengths, Weaknesses, Opportunities, and Threats

SYMBOL: a sign or trademark designed to represent a brand

| see illustration p.93

93

THE FAMOUS NIKE SYMBOL

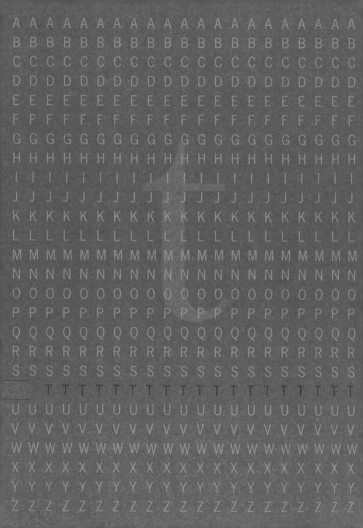

TACTIC: an expedient maneuver used in support of a strategy

TAGLINE: a sentence, phrase, or word used to summarize a market position, such as Mini's "Let's motor" and Taco Bell's "Think outside the bun" | also see p.78 positioning | also see p.89 slogan | also see p.105 why-to-buy message

TARGET MARKET: the group of customers a company has decided to serve | also see p.88 segmentation

TEAM DYNAMICS: the psychological factors that influence collaboration, including trust, fear respect, and company politics

| see *Unstuck*, Keith Yamashita and Sandra Spataro

THOUGHT LEADER: a brand that leads the market in influential ideas, though not necessarily in market share, such as Apple Computer

TIPPING POINT: a leverage point in the evolution of a market or society where a small effort can yield a surprisingly large result, not unlike "the straw that breaks the camel's back"

| see *The Tipping Point*, Malcolm Gladwell

TOUCHPOINT: any place where people come in contact with a brand, including product use, packaging, advertising, editorial, movies, store environments, company employees, and casual conversation

TRADE DRESS: the colors, shapes, typefaces, page treatments, and other visual properties that create a recognizable "face" for a brand

| also see p.20 brand identity | also see p.59 kit of parts

TRADEMARK: a name and/or symbol that indicates a source of goods or services and prevents confusion in the marketplace; a legally protectable form of intellectual property

| see *Designing Brand Identity*, by Alina Wheeler

TRIBAL BRAND: a brand with a cult-like following, such as Harley-Davidson, eBay, or American Idol

TURFISMO: the tendency of managers to protect their autonomy at the expense of collaboration

TV-INDUSTRIAL COMPLEX: the dominant system for launching and sustaining national brands during the last half of the 20th century, now weakened by the spread of new media and tribal brands

| see p.97 tribal brand | see *Purple Cow*, Seth Godin

A A A A A A A A A A A A A A A A A A A A A A
B B B B B B B B B B B B B B B B B B B B B B
C C C C C C C C C C C C C C C C C C C C C C
D D D D D D D D D D D D D D D D D D D D D D
E E E E E E E E E E E E E E E E E E E E E E
F F F F F F F F F F F F F F F F F F F F F F
G G G G G G G G G G G G G G G G G G G G G G
H H H H H H H H H H H H H H H H H H H H H H
I I I I I I I I I I I I I I I I I I I I I I
J J J J J J J J J J J J J J J J J J J J J J
K K K K K K K K K K K K K K K K K K K K K K
L L L L L L L L L L L L L L L L L L L L L L
M M M M M M M M M M M M M M M M M M M M M M
N N N N N N N N N N N N N N N N N N N N N N
O O O O O O O O O O O O O O O O O O O O O O
P P P P P P P P P P P P P P P P P P P P P P
Q Q Q Q Q Q Q Q Q Q Q Q Q Q Q Q Q Q Q Q Q Q
R R R R R R R R R R R R R R R R R R R R R R
S S S S S S S S S S S S S S S S S S S S S S
T T T T T T T T T T T T T T T T T T T T T T
U U U U U U U U U U U U U U U U U U U U
V V V V V V V V V V V V V V V V V V V V V V
W W W W W W W W W W W W W W W W W W W W W W
X X X X X X X X X X X X X X X X X X X X X X
Y Y Y Y Y Y Y Y Y Y Y Y Y Y Y Y Y Y Y Y Y Y
Z Z Z Z Z Z Z Z Z Z Z Z Z Z Z Z Z Z Z Z Z Z

USP: the Unique Selling Proposition of a product or service, as championed by advertising executive Rosser Reeves in the 1950s; a type of differentiation | see p.38 differentiation

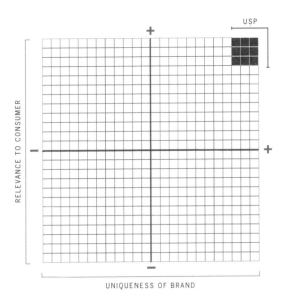

USP

RELEVANCE TO CONSUMER

UNIQUENESS OF BRAND

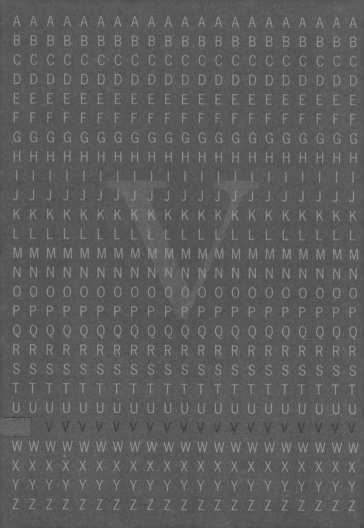

VALIDATION: customer approval or feedback for a proposed message, concept, or prototype see p.81 prototype

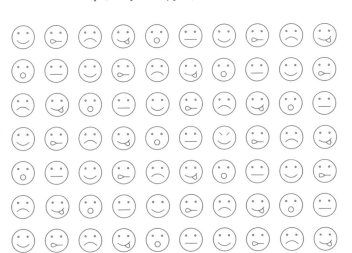

VALUE PROPOSITION: a set of benefits, including functional, emotional, and self-expressive benefits

VICIOUS CIRCLE: in brand strategy, a death spiral that leads from a lack of differentiation to lower prices, to smaller profit margins, to fewer available resources, to less innovation, to even less differentiation, and finally to commoditization | the opposite of virtuous circle see p.68

VIRAL MARKETING: a technique by which social networks are used to spread ideas or messages, through the use of affiliate programs, co-branding, e-mails, and link exchanges on-line, or off-line, through use of word-of-mouth advertising and memes

see p.67 meme | see *Unleashing the Ideavirus*, Seth Godin

VIRTUAL AGENCY: a team of specialist firms that work together to build a brand, coined by Susan Rockrise of Intel; also called an *IMT* or *metateam*

see p.54 IMT | see p.68 metateam | also see p.51 Hollywood model

VIRTUOUS CIRCLE: the opposite of a vicious circle; a growth spiral of growth that leads from differentiation, to higher prices, to larger profit margins, to more available resources, to more innovation, to further differentiation, and then to a sustainable competitive advantage

VISION: the story a leader tells about where the organization is going; the aspirations of a company that drive future growth

VIVID DESCRIPTION: a vibrant, clear, and engaging vision of what it will be like to achieve a **BHAG**

see p.9 BHAG | see *Built to Last*, Jim Collins and Jerry Porras

VOICE: the unique personality of a company as expressed by its verbal and written communications; the verbal dimension of a brand personality

see p.24 brand personality

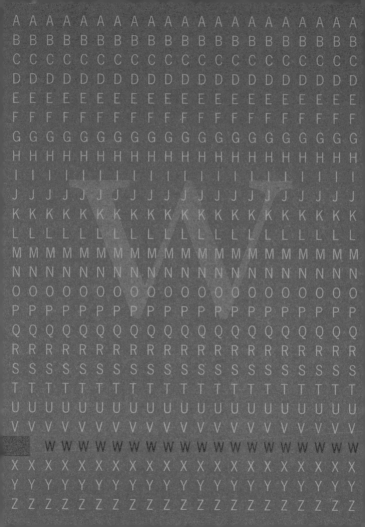

WORD-OF-MOUTH ADVERTISING:
a form of communication in which
people voluntarily promote a brand,
resulting in a brand with a high level
of authenticity | see p.6 authenticity

| see p.102 viral marketing

WORDMARK: the brand name as
represented by a distinctive typeface
or lettering style; a logotype | see p.62 logotype

Brooks Brothers

WHY-TO-BUY MESSAGE: the most
compelling reason to buy a product,
often stated as a tagline | see p.95 tagline

A A A A A A A A A A A A A A A A A A A A A
B B B B B B B B B B B B B B B B B B B B B
C C C C C C C C C C C C C C C C C C C C C
D D D D D D D D D D D D D D D D D D D D D
E E E E E E E E E E E E E E E E E E E E E
F F F F F F F F F F F F F F F F F F F F F
G G G G G G G G G G G G G G G G G G G G G
H H H H H H H H H H H H H H H H H H H H H
I I I I I I I I I I I I I I I I I I I I I
J J J J J J J J J J J J J J J J J J J J J
K K K K K K K K K K K K K K K K K K K K K
L L L L L L L L L L L L L L L L L L L L L
M M M M M M M M M M M M M M M M M M M M M
N N N N N N N N N N N N N N N N N N N N N
O O O O O O O O O O O O O O O O O O O O O
P P P P P P P P P P P P P P P P P P P P P
Q Q Q Q Q Q Q Q Q Q Q Q Q Q Q Q Q Q Q Q Q
R R R R R R R R R R R R R R R R R R R R R
S S S S S S S S S S S S S S S S S S S S S
T T T T T T T T T T T T T T T T T T T T T
U U U U U U U U U U U U U U U U U U U U U
V V V V V V V V V V V V V V V V V V V V V
W W W W W W W W W W W W W W W W W W W W W
X X X X X X X X X X X X X X X X X X X
Y Y Y Y Y Y Y Y Y Y Y Y Y Y Y Y Y Y Y Y Y
Z Z Z Z Z Z Z Z Z Z Z Z Z Z Z Z Z Z Z Z Z

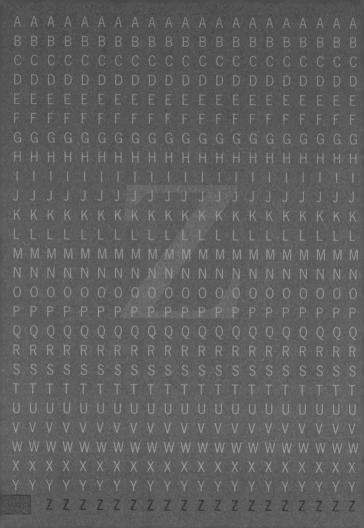

ZAG: a disruptive innovation that
 yields a competitive advantage; the
 differentiating idea that drives a
 charismatic brand | see p.29 charismatic brand

| see "When everybody zigs, zag", *The Brand Gap*, Marty Neumeier

COLOPHON

The Dictionary of Brand was edited by
Marty Neumeier of Neutron in San Francisco
(www.neutronllc.com), and designed by
Ann Willoughby, Deb Tagtalianidis, and
Ryan Jones of Willoughby Design Group in
Kansas City (www.willoughbydesign.com).

It was printed by Metropolitan Fine Printers in
Vancouver, B.C. (www.metprinters.com). The
imaging was created with 10-micron Staccato™,
screening and the binding was Smyth-sewn with
a draw-on cover.

The paper is 120lb Carnival Duplex White/Red
Cover and 100lb Carnival Vellum Stellar White
Text, kindly contributed by SMART Papers
(www.smartpapers.com).

The Dictionary of Brand was produced using
Adobe InDesign and Adobe Illustrator on an
Apple Macintosh platform. The typefaces are
Baskerville and News Gothic.

ACKNOWLEDGMENT

SMART Papers values this partnership with AIGA and the design community, and looks forward to a future of collaboration that strives for excellence in printed communications.

SMART Papers draws on a rich 109-year heritage of premium papermaking, and is located in Hamilton, Ohio where Kromekote, the world's leading cast-coated paper, was developed.

SMART Papers offers some of the industry's most proven, well known, and valuable brands including Kromekote, Knightkote Matte, Carnival, and Benefit, plus the new SMART Digital line of both coated and uncoated papers. Their selection of premium cast-coated, matte-coated and uncoated text, cover, and writing papers offers advantages of brand quality, choice, and reliability at a value price.

SMART Papers is proud to contribute all paper for *The Dictionary of Brand* and intends to be a resource for designers by providing products, service, and information on paper as well as printing that promises to be refreshing, relevant, and educational.

For more information on SMART Papers visit www.smartpapers.com.

NOTES ON THE DICTIONARY

From the outset we accepted that the language of brand is a moving target. While most dictionary editors try for timelessness, we had no such option, since useful brand terms are being minted daily. Instead, we tried for universality, believing if we could reduce the terms and their definitions to those that might be practical for a wide range of disciplines, we'd realize our goal of establishing a shared language.

You'll notice that some of the terms are fairly long in the tooth, such as *trademark*, while others seem as if they were born yesterday, such as *avatar*. We tried not to discriminate, since both types of terms are useful in today's brand conversations.

We also tried to redefine certain words that are widely understood, but needed a tweak in light of recent advances. For example, the term media advertising is defined as "one-way messages designed to sell, persuade, or create awareness of a brand through public communication channels." The tweak here is "one-way", since brand builders now realize they have alternative tools, such as buzz creation, viral marketing, and online interaction, that offer two-way communication.

This in no way diminishes the power of advertising—on the contrary, it serves to focus it.

Most dictionary editors also try for completeness. For example, the *Concise Oxford Dictionary* contains 240,000 terms, and a single term may have dozens of meanings. We've taken the opposite approach, aiming for the least number of terms, and a maximum of two definitions each. While the first edition of *The Dictionary of Brand* contains only 221 terms, we take comfort in the knowledge that Shakespeare wrote all his plays and sonnets with only a 5,000-word vocabulary, including small words like *to*, *be*, *or*, and *not*.

Finally, we tried to employ internal logic in our choice of terms. For example, since we included *primacy effect*, we also included its unidentical twin, *recency effect*. Within each term's definition, we made a reference to the other term. You'll also notice that wherever one term is included in another's definition, we added a footnote with the page number of that definition.

We consider the dictionary a work in progress. If there are definitions you disagree with, or terms you'd like to add, please e-mail your comments to marty@neutronllc.com.

DICTIONARY ADVISORY COUNCIL

Jeremy Bullmore, WPP

Hugh Dubberly, Dubberly Design Office

Tom Kelley, IDEO

Davis Masten, Cheskin Research

Seth Godin, author

Al Ries, author

Susan Rockrise, Intel

Michael Schrage, author

Alina Wheeler, author

Stone Yamashita Partners